It Takes Less Than One Minute To Suit Up For The Lord

THIS BOOK BELONGS TO

BJ -

You have been a
blessing in my life.
Thanks for your leadership
mentoring, friendship
and living your
faith. May God
always bless you!
9-27-12 Pz

It Takes Less Than
One
Minute
To Suit Up For
The Lord

Ken Blanchard
Co-Author of *The One Minute Manager*®

**Executive
Books**

It Takes Less Than One Minute to Suit Up for the Lord

Published by
Executive Books
206 West Allen Street
Mechanicsburg, PA 17055
717-766-9499   800-233-2665
Fax: 717-766-6565
www.ExecutiveBooks.com

Copyright © 2004 by Ken Blanchard

ISBN: 0-937539-88-0

Printed in the United States of America

Cover design and interior layout by Gregory A. Dixon

This book is dedicated to:

Dorothy Blanchard
Norman Vincent Peale
Bob Buford
Phil Hodges
Bill Hybels

My mom, Dorothy Blanchard, always had a beautiful spirit and great faith in the Lord. Throughout her ninety-five years on this planet she was an inspiration as well as a spiritual guide for me and everyone whose life she touched. Mom used to always ask me why I never wrote a book by myself. She finally got her wish when I wrote *We Are the Beloved,* the first edition of this little book. In fact, one of the joys in the last few months of her life was having me read from this text. I miss you, Mom.

When I finished the first draft of *We Are the Beloved,* I over-nighted a copy to Norman Vincent Peale. At ninety-five he was in poor health and fading fast, but I hoped he would get to see it because Norman had played such an important role in my spiritual journey. When we were working together on *The Power of Ethical Management,* I wasn't a believer. Yet Norman kept telling me, "Ken, the

Lord has always had you on His team; you just haven't suited up yet." It was that statement that inspired the title for this new edition.

Ruth Peale told me Norman had already lost consciousness when the book arrived, but she rushed it to his bedside and said, "Norman, look what Ken has written. And he dedicated it to you." As only Ruth would think to say, she told me, "Ken, I feel he knew what I was saying." I hope so, because Norman Vincent Peale's positive thinking ministry made a difference in my life and the lives of generations of people who were profoundly influenced by his sermons, speeches, radio shows, television appearances and books. While he never got to read this book, Norman's whole life was dedicated to helping others think positively and realize the power that comes with "suiting up" for the Lord.

Bob Buford—coauthor of *Half Time* and founder of The Leadership Network—Phil Hodges, long-time friend and co-founder with me of the Center for FaithWalk Leadership, and Bill Hybels, senior pastor of Willow Creek Community Church, also played key roles in my suiting up. I will be talking about them throughout this little book. I feel so blessed to still have them in my life.

TABLE OF CONTENTS

Acknowledgments

Bibliography

About the Author

Services Available

INTRODUCTION

A number of years ago I started emphasizing the importance of self-esteem in my leadership and management lectures and seminars. I did this because it was becoming clearer to me that managers today, in a world demanding an empowered workforce, have to be more like cheerleaders, supporters, and encouragers than the judges, critics, and evaluators they have been in the past. Yet, I realized that it is almost impossible for people who don't feel good about themselves to play these new roles. I began to wonder if effective leadership doesn't actually begin on the inside and move out. After all, only people who genuinely like themselves can build up others without feeling it takes something away from themselves.

My sudden concern with self-worth coincided with a renewed spiritual interest. In exploring my own spirituality, I began to sense that the quickest and most powerful way to significantly enhance one's self-worth and make oneself more loving was to awaken spiritually.

I say "awaken" because I have come to believe that all of us develop amnesia after we are born. We begin to forget from where we came. We start to lose touch with home base. In the first *Chicken Soup for the Soul,* Jack Canfield and Mark Victor Hansen included a beautiful story about a little girl by the name of Sachi. The story is all about this amnesia. Soon after her brother was born, little Sachi began to ask her parents to leave her alone with the new baby. They worried that like most four-year-olds, she might feel jealous and want to hit or shake him, so they said no. But she showed no signs of jealousy. She treated the baby with kindness, and her pleas to be left alone with him became more urgent. Her parents decided to allow it.

Elated, she went into the baby's room and shut the door, but it opened a crack—enough for her curious parents to peek in and listen. They saw little Sachi walk quietly up to her baby brother, put her face close to his and say quietly, "Baby, tell me what God is like. I'm starting to forget."

It takes us different lengths of time to get back home—to accept that we come from the best lineage there is and have the unconditional love of the Father—the Master of the House. We have "God-esteem" which is more powerful than "self-esteem."

This book is not about persuading you to believe in God. I think most people believe in God. I once heard it said that not to believe in a Creator makes as much sense as saying the unabridged dictionary is the result of an explosion in a print shop. My hope is to clear up your amnesia and help you remember what you once knew in childlike innocence: that there is something or someone out there bigger than you who has a divine purpose for your life. The first step in any spiritual journey is a longing for home, a yearning to reconnect with something bigger than yourself.

The focus in this book is on suiting up—deliberately accepting on faith God's unconditional love for us as manifested in His gift of grace through His Son, Jesus Christ. In sports, you suit up when it's time to play. Once you get in uniform, you still might not get sent into the game, but you're ready if the coach needs you. In my travels, I find that most people today are restless and hungry to get "into the game" and experience the deeper meaning of their lives. They just don't know where to start.

Rather than trying to convince you what to do, I'd simply like to share what I believe is an incredibly good deal. When I found out Peter Drucker—the real guru in my field—was a Christian, I asked him why. Peter, with his characteristic, straightforward approach, said, "There is no better deal. Who else has grace?" As I'll reveal in this book, grace answers the questions about self-esteem and self-worth once and for all; for it's the realization that once you receive the Lord's forgiveness through grace, you have all the love you will ever need. You have God-esteem. No amount of striving for approval or achieving greater and greater things will give you more love and acceptance than you already have.

That's why I titled the first edition of this book *We Are the Beloved*—because you already are loved, with no strings attached. Even if you decide that you cannot yet accept God's love, you are still loved by Him. You just miss out on the daily joy of realizing you have the most important teammate you could ever want.

This deal is also incredibly good because it satisfies our longing for meaning and purpose. It lends to everyday life a quality that I think most of us are desperate for today—the sense that we're on our own hero's journey; that spiritually speaking, life can be viewed as a magic carpet ride.

This little book was originally written as a Christmas 1994 gift for the most important people in my life—my family and friends. But so much has happened in my spiritual life in the last decade that it made sense to update my story. Rick Warren, author of *A Purpose Driven Life* and senior pastor of Saddleback Community Church in Orange County, California, compares the spiritual journey of a Christian to the four bases on a baseball field. Rick says that getting to first base involves commitment to the Lord by confessing our sins and acknowledging God's grace. Getting to second base is all about growing in our knowledge of the Lord through solitude, prayer, study of scripture and fellowship. The trip from second to third base involves serving the Lord through some ministry. We round third and head for home when we are able to recruit for the Lord and share our faith comfortably with others on a continuous basis.

I've spent a good deal of time over the last ten years growing in my knowledge of the Lord. While I'm far from finished there, in recent years I have begun to focus more energy on serving the Lord and sharing my faith with others.

I turned sixty-five this year along with a bunch of my old buddies. A number of them are retiring and are wondering when I am going to slow down. I talked this over with Zig Ziglar, a legendary motivational teacher and author of *See You at the Top*, who is in his late seventies. Zig reminded me that there is no mention of retirement in the Bible. In fact, except for Jesus, David, Mary and the disciples, few people under seventy made much of a contribution. Zig said, "I'm refiring, not retiring." I like that concept, especially when I take into consideration my involvement in recent years with the Center for FaithWalk Leadership and our Lead Like Jesus movement. Now I am really having a chance to serve the Lord and share my faith with others.

It is through the urging of my family and friends that I agreed to share the original story of my spiritual journey more widely. It is with this same motivation that I do it again. I share my story not because I think it is so extraordinary. In fact, I'm still en route, with much yet to learn about God's unconditional love. I share it because I hope it helps some of you who are thinking seriously about accepting His love, together with all the God-esteem, power, and freedom that it brings.

KEN BLANCHARD
FALL 2004

MY JOURNEY

The grace of our Lord was poured out on me abundantly, along with the faith and love that are in Christ Jesus.

1 Timothy 1:14

EARLY RELIGIOUS BACKGROUND

I grew up in New Rochelle, New York. I was named after a Presbyterian minister. Bob Hartley was the pastor of the First Presbyterian Church my parents attended, and his ministry had such a big impact on them that when I was born they gave me the middle name, Hartley. I never got to know Bob Hartley; he died of a heart attack when I was five. But in later years I learned that my coauthor and friend, Norman Vincent Peale, had been a classmate of Reverend Hartley at divinity school.

Over the years my mom repeatedly told me a story about Bob Hartley that will give you a sense of the kind of person he was as well as what an example of "the greatest generation" my father was. My father grew up in Highland Falls, New York, a small town just outside the gate of West Point, the United States Military Academy. My father loved West Point and all the pomp and circumstance surrounding it. But when he graduated from high school his father, a doctor in town, said, "Son, I think you should go away to school."

Since that was the case and he couldn't go to West Point, my father decided to go to the Naval Academy in Annapolis, Maryland.

When he graduated in 1924 from the Naval Academy, my father found that in a world that believed it had just fought the "war to end all wars," there was little need for naval officers. So after his senior cruise, he entered Harvard Business School, where he majored in finance and ended up working in New York City. In the early 1940s he was being groomed for a vice-presidency with National City Bank when one day he came home and said to my mom, "Honey, I quit today."

"You did what?" my mother replied.

"I quit," Dad said. "I told you when we got married that if the country ever got in trouble, I felt I owed it something. Hitler is already a threat to world peace, and it's only a matter of time until Japan gets into the fray, so I reenlisted."

This was quite a shock for my mom. I was one year old, my sister Sandy was three, and just when Dad was starting to make some good money, he opted for a lieutenant's salary in the Navy. Mom went along with it as graciously as she could.

In spite of my father's zest for action, his first assignment was the Brooklyn Navy Yard. Pearl Harbor came along, and still no change. When it looked like he'd be stuck in dry dock for the duration of the war, he called one of his former classmates—who happened to be head of the Naval Bureau of Personnel in Washington, D.C.—and asked him what he had for an old-timer with no experience. A week later his friend called him back.

"Ted, all I have for a guy with your background is a suicide group going into the Marshall Islands," he said.

My dad jumped at it—without telling my mom about the suicide part, of course. They gave him command of twelve LCIs (landing craft infantry). With only small guns to protect themselves, Dad's units were responsible for protecting the marines and frogmen (the SEALS of today) heading into the island beaches that were held down by the Japanese. My dad's friend had been right in calling this a suicide mission; it was one of the most vulnerable positions in the campaign. Seventy percent of Dad's men were killed or wounded. His ships were so close to the beaches that Dad's picture was in *Time* magazine one week: it showed him conducting funeral services for some of his men who'd been hit by explosives that fell short after they were launched from our big ships.

As my dad's ships headed into Saipan for what was expected to be the biggest battle in the Pacific, he wrote to Mom's oldest brother Fred: "Chances of me making it out of this campaign are very slim. I know if anything happens, you'll watch over Dorothy and the kids." To my mother he wrote a second letter, telling her: "Everything is fine here on maneuvers. The only trouble we're encountering is the heat."

Through some strange accident of fate, Dad got the two letters mixed up. My uncle got Mom's "maneuvers" letter, and she got the one about the low probability of survival. Devastated, she ran to the phone and called Reverend Hartley. In ten minutes he was at our front door with a big smile on his face.

"What a blessing!" he exclaimed.

Mom thought the reverend had lost his mind. "What do you mean 'what a blessing'?"

"It's God's sign that Ted's going to be okay," he said. "The letters getting mixed up means that we've been getting too complacent and not praying enough."

When I told that story about his divinity school classmate to Norman Vincent Peale, he said, "Now that's good preaching!" Whether it was good preaching or just praying enough, it worked because my dad came home safe and sound.

Soon after the war, Bob Hartley died. We continued to go to the First Presbyterian Church until I was in junior high. Then we moved to the First Methodist Church where a classmate's father, Harrison Davis, was the minister. Not only was he a good preacher, he was a wonderful guy as well. And besides, they had a better basketball team than the Presbyterian Church had.

Throughout my high school days, I was a regular churchgoer, active in Youth Fellowship. Then I went off to college at Cornell University in Ithaca, in upstate New York. Under the university's hands-off policy with regard to student religious observances, I started to drift away. With studies and an increasingly busy campus life, I never really found a church to attend in Ithaca.

The summer after I graduated I started to date Margie McKee, who was a fourth generation Cornellian. We were both working in the Ithaca area. I was working as a dorm counselor for the National Science Foundation and playing a lot of golf, while Margie, a speech therapy major, was working at a special camp for handicapped kids. Margie had gone out with a number of my good friends, and they all said that she was the greatest. In fact, I first called her for a date as a favor to one of my friends. He'd been dating her and was concerned she might be lonely by herself in Ithaca that summer.

When I arrived to pick Margie up for our date I said to her, "Tell me, why are you working out here with all these handicapped kids?" She spoke with such love and compassion about her work with those kids that I fell in love with her during the seven-mile ride into town. By the end of the evening, I was already worrying about how to tell my friend the bad news. Luckily Margie was thinking the same thing. We were married a year later, after Margie's graduation from Cornell. My friend named his first child Ken, so he couldn't have been that mad.

The first year we were married we lived in Hamilton, New York, while I finished my master's degree at Colgate University and Margie worked as a speech therapist for the Madison County schools. When we returned to Cornell the next year for my doctorate and Margie's master's degree, we met a fabulous young minister from the First Presbyterian Church in Ithaca by the name of Paul Clark. He got us gung ho for church again, and we even volunteered to run the junior high school program.

In 1966 we headed out to Ohio University in Athens for my first job as administrative assistant to the dean of the College of Business Administration. Our son, Scott, was just a baby, and Margie was pregnant with Debbie. In Athens we met a wonderful minister at the Methodist church in town and began to be active in that church.

This was the late sixties, a time of much student unrest. The Kent State incident occurred right down the road. We had our own little incident of disillusionment that fit right in with the times. Our minister friend sympathized with students; he was right up front at all the protests and marches. That didn't go over well with his conservative southeastern Ohio congregation. They fired him in what seemed to us a most un-Christian manner.

Disillusionment Sets In

Anger and disillusionment came crashing in on us. We thought, *If that's what Christianity is all about, forget it.* We dropped out. Like so many people, if we went to church at all, it was only on Christmas and Easter. That went on for fifteen years. Unfortunately, since these were the key growing-up years for Scott and Debbie, faith was not a big part of our family's life. In fact, if you'd threatened some punishment for Scott and Debbie unless they could recite the Lord's Prayer, I'm afraid you'd have had to dole out the punishment. We had drifted that far away from the church.

In 1970, we moved to Amherst, Massachusetts where I taught at the University of Massachusetts and Margie worked on her doctorate in communication studies. After six years there, we went to San Diego for a one-year sabbatical leave. Living for a few months in California where sunshine is cheap, we realized that summer in Massachusetts was two weeks of bad skating. As a result, we decided to stay on the West Coast and start our own company, Blanchard Training and Development, Inc. (BTD).

Then *The One Minute Manager®* happened. Spencer Johnson, my coauthor, and I met at a cocktail party in November 1980. Spencer was a children's book writer. He had coauthored a wonderful children's series called *Value Tales*. The series included *The Value of Curiosity: The Story of Christopher Columbus; The Value of Believing in Yourself: The Story of Louis Pasteur; The Value of a Sense of Humor: The Story of Will Rogers,* etc. Margie met Spencer first. She hand-carried him over to me and said, "Why don't you two work on a children's book for managers? They won't read anything else."

Spencer was working on a one minute parenting book with a psychiatrist. When he explained his approach to parenting, I told him I had been teaching those kinds of things to managers for years. So I invited him to a seminar I was giving the following Monday at the Rancho Bernardo Inn in San Diego. He came and sat in the back of the room and laughed throughout the day. At the end of the seminar, he ran up to me and said, "Forget parenting! Let's go for managers." That was the birth of *The One Minute Manager*.

We had a first draft ready for people to read in a Winnebago on the way to the Rose Bowl on December 31. We self-published *The One Minute Manager* by May 1981 and introduced it at the National Restaurant Association Convention in Chicago later that month. Dick Gaven, a friend and fraternity brother of mine, was the Director of

Education for the association at that time and got us on the program. Within twenty minutes after the session, we had sold almost a thousand copies of the book in the back of the room. During the next year, with almost no publicity, we sold 20,000 copies, mainly to our Blanchard Training and Development customers.

When Spencer and our literary agent, Margret McBride, went to New York for meetings in January 1982, they found that several publishers were interested in the book. But the person who impressed us the most was Larry Hughes, president of William Morrow. Two weeks after its publication by William Morrow in September, *The One Minute Manager* was on the *New York Times* bestseller list, where it stayed for the next three years.

Openness to God

Several months after the book came out I got a call from Phil Hodges, a longtime friend from Cornell, wanting to know if we could get together for a walk on the beach. Phil was a top labor-relations officer for Xerox, working in the Los Angeles area. He had turned his life over to the Lord several years before and had been praying for me ever since. When we took our walk, Phil asked, "Ken, why do you think *The One Minute Manager* is such a runaway bestseller? Do you think it's because you're a better writer than anyone else or that you're smarter than most people?"

I said, "No, Hodge, I don't think that at all. I've thought a lot about it. The success of *The One Minute*

Manager is too unbelievable for me to take any credit. I think God is involved."

Phil grinned. "Thank God," he said, "I hoped you would have that attitude."

That meeting with Phil Hodges marked the renewal of my spiritual journey, which had begun when I was a little guy being taken to church by my parents. Afterward, Phil kept calling me, sending me things to read, pushing me to think about my relationship with Christ.

In 1985 my journey got a boost from two occurrences. First, Larry Hughes called and asked, "Ken, would you be interested in writing a book with Norman Vincent Peale?"

My initial response was, "Is he still alive?" My parents had gone to Norman's church before I was born.

Larry said, "Not only is he still alive but Norman and his wife, Ruth, are two of the most special people in the world." That was the beginning of the wonderful relationship Margie and I developed with the Peales and our journey to suit up.

Discovering the Meaning of Grace

The second occurrence happened when Margie and I met Bob and Linda Buford. Bob was a member of the Young Presidents Organization (YPO). In those days to be a YPO member you had to become president of your organization before you were forty years old and have a minimum of $5 million in sales or budget and at least fifty people working for you. It was a group of YPOers who had convinced Margie and me not to go back to the university after our sabbatical leave and to stay in California and start our own company.

I'd met Bob Buford casually before at some YPO events where Margie and I had been asked to speak, so I knew of his deep faith and commitment to a personal ministry to help support and coach the ministers of large growth churches.

On the way to a YPO conference in Mexico City, we saw the Bufords between flights in the Admirals Club at the Dallas-Fort Worth Airport. When we got on the plane, I discovered that Bob's seat was across the aisle from mine. During our chatting, I went to get something in my wallet and found tucked away among the bills a little booklet about Christianity called The *Four Spiritual Laws* written by Bill Bright, Founder of Campus Crusade for Christ. Phil Hodges' daughter LeeAnne had gotten it at Sunday school and Phil had given it to me to read. I don't recall putting it in my wallet, but there it was! Now that Bob Buford was sitting next to me, finding that booklet took on new meaning.

I said, "Bob, this booklet is in my wallet for some reason. Maybe it means we should talk about Christianity. I have a few questions I'd like to ask you."

"I'll do my best, Ken," said Bob. "But remember. I'm only a layman."

So there in the sky we started going over the booklet together. The first spiritual law stated: "God loves you and offers a wonderful plan for your life."

I could buy that one all right, but the second law was where my questions started. It contended that we are all sinners. That had always bothered me for two reasons. First, I don't like labels. If you call somebody a "sinner" they really get their back up. Second, from my standpoint as a humanist, the concept of original sin was too negative. I'd always thought that people should be considered to have "original potentiality." That is, as human beings we have the potential to be either good or bad.

When I asked Bob about original sin he said, "Let me ask you a question, Ken. Do you think you're as good as God?"

"Of course not," I answered. "The concept of God has to do with perfection."

"Okay. On a scale of 1 to 100, let's give God 100. We'll give Mother Teresa 90, and an ax murderer 5. Ken, you're a decent sort and are trying to help others. I'll give you 75. Now the special thing about Christianity is that God sent Jesus to earth to make up the difference between you and 100."

That appealed to me. I'd never heard grace explained that way. Ask anybody, "on a scale of 1 to 100, with 100 being perfection, where would you rate yourself?" Nobody would say 100. We all know that we fall short of perfection. What a better way to explain grace than calling people sinners.

"Before you get too excited," Bob continued, "Let me give you the whole story. A lot of people don't like the fact that the ax murderer gets the same shot at the ball as

Mother Teresa, but that's what grace is all about. It's not about deeds; it's about faith. If you accept Jesus Christ as your Savior, no matter what your past has been, He rids you of your sins and this makes up the difference between you and 100."

For the rest of the flight I peppered Bob with questions. As we deplaned in Mexico City, Bob said, "I've got a friend I want you to meet who can answer your questions much better than I can. His name is Bill Hybels, and he's minister of one of the fastest-growing churches in the country, the Willow Creek Community Church outside of Chicago. And another thing—he's speaking at this conference. If it's okay, I'm going to see to it that you guys have lunch together."

I didn't know Bill Hybels from a hole in the ground. But I later learned that if you get caught in his jaws as a non-believer, you are in deep trouble. Bill and I did have lunch, and he later described our conversation in his inspirational book *Seven Wonders of the Spiritual World*. I led off with the same question I'd asked Bob Buford: "Why original sin? It's too negative."

Bill said, "Ken, let me explain the difference between Christianity and religion. The main difference is in how they're spelled. Religion is spelled 'do.' That means there are all kinds of things you must do to receive the Lord's grace. Religion stresses what you need to do to deserve God's favor. What new leaf can you turn over? What new commitment can you make to get yourself right with God? The problem with religion and the 'do' philosophy is that most people quit because they never know when enough is enough. Suppose you do 2,500 good things in your life, and then you get to judgment day and the Lord says, 'That's not bad but you needed to do 3,000.'"

Bill went on to say, "Christianity is spelled 'done.' The Lord sent Jesus to earth to take care of it. You can't perform well enough or do enough good things to get into heaven. The only entry is by admitting you are a sinner (that is, falling short of a 100 in Bob Buford's terms) and accepting Jesus as your Savior. He is the only one who can cleanse your past. You cannot do it yourself." Bill talked about a personal relationship with Christ, something I had not experienced even in the days when I was active in church. "Not only can He save you, but He can become your guide and your friend. He can energize your life and transform it."

The simplicity of Bill's explanation hit me. I had attended church for years, but I had never heard the message of grace with such clarity and power. All my misgivings about original sin were stripped away. I wasn't a bad person; I just fell short of God's perfection and by accepting Jesus as my Savior could I be given grace. Then I could reach 100 and be right with the Lord through God's forgiveness of my imperfections.

When I asked Bill how I could accept grace, he said, "It's easy for a One Minute Manager. All you have to do is bow your head and say, 'Lord, I can't save myself; I am a sinner. I fall short of 100. I accept Jesus Christ as my Savior and bridge between me and You. From this day forward I turn my life over to Him.'"

While I was excited and could feel the adrenaline pumping, I was reluctant to jump in with both feet. And Bill could sense it. I told him I was worried about a commitment to Christ because I was afraid I wouldn't be able to follow through. "I'll fail," I said.

Bill took out a pen and wrote the words "commit" and "follow through" on a paper napkin. Then he said, "Please don't ever use those two words. Becoming a Christian is not about committing and following through. God knows you can't keep your commitment. God knows you can't follow through. Christianity is a matter of two different words: *receive* and *trust*. Romans 6:23 says, 'For the wages of sin is death, but the free gift of God is eternal life in Jesus Christ our Lord.'

"What is a gift?" Bill asked.

I said, "Something you receive."

"That's right," said Bill. "Salvation, regeneration, newness of life, and forgiveness of sin are things that can only be received. And once you receive grace, once you receive forgiveness, you've got them. Your next step is to trust God and say, 'I don't know what all this means, and I don't know where I am going, but I am going to trust You each step of the way and see what happens.'"

My lunch with Bill really made me think about Christianity. But I still wasn't ready to suit up yet. I just wasn't ready to let go of my life and hand it over to God.

After our lunch together, whenever I saw Bill at the conference he would smile and say, "Receive and trust."

Suiting Up

It's hard for human beings to let go completely. We think we can figure everything out for ourselves. I kept on thinking about what Bob and Bill had said, but it wasn't until almost a year later that I acknowledged I was seriously ready to suit up.

It occurred after Margie and I turned over the presidency of Blanchard Training and Development to an individual who had more business experience than we did and who felt he could move our company forward. As it turned out, we didn't always agree on some basic values. No matter how much we tried to see the world as he did, it just didn't help. He had a high need to control and a win-lose attitude toward most things. His approach might have been appropriate in a different organization, but in our company it was a disaster.

Margie and I tried everything to resolve this conflict, but no matter what we tried, it just didn't help. It became clear that things were just not working out. What was worse, I felt powerless to do anything about it.

One evening, Margie and I decided to meet at a local restaurant for dinner and talk about our options.

Earlier that day, I recalled a conversation I'd had with Bill Hybels. We'd once talked about my work as a consultant, helping executives solve sticky problems that came up in their organizations. Bill had said, "Ken, I can't understand why you won't receive the gift of God's grace, because if you do, you get three top consultants for the price of one—the Father, who created it all; the Son, who taught us all we should know and how to do it; and the Holy Spirit, who is our day-to-day operational manager. When you suit up for the Lord and accept Jesus as your Savior, the Holy Spirit jumps in and offers sure guidance whenever you're stuck. That's a good deal, Blanchard."

As my dinner meeting with Margie approached, I thought, *Man, why am I trying to solve this all by myself?* Suddenly, I knew what I was going to do. A wave of tremendous relief flowed through me. I bowed my head and said, "Lord, I can't make it to 100 by myself. I can't solve problems like this without Your help. I admit that I need You and recognize my vulnerability. I accept Jesus as my Savior and the bridge between You and me." The moment I said these words, a great peace came over me.

That feeling was still with me when I walked into the restaurant to meet Margie. She took one look at me and said, "What happened to you? You look so relaxed and calm." Then I told her what I had done and how I was going to trust God to give me the wisdom and strength to deal with the problem presented by our president. Later, I phoned Bill Hybels and left a message on his answering machine that I had received Christ and was ready to trust my life to Him. I also got great joy when I told my Mom, Bob Buford, Phil Hodges, and Norman Vincent Peale.

The True Reward for Suiting Up

I would like to report that God solved this business problem with some miraculous stroke of His hand, but it didn't happen that way, and I've learned that it seldom does. Yet I believe His hand was on me when a few days later I attended a meeting of the American Society for Training and Development, at which a friend and colleague, Tom Crum, was speaking. Tom is the author of *The Magic of Conflict* and an expert in aikido, an oriental form of self-defense that stresses using the energy of your opponent to defeat that person. Through Tom's dynamic demonstrations and his way of involving all participants in practice, he showed us how to neutralize an attack by responding in ways other than resisting it.

"If someone goes to punch you," Tom said, "don't try to block the punch. When you do that, you are using resistance—your own power and strength against the attacker's. That sets up a win-lose confrontation." Tom showed how to step aside with an accepting and pivoting movement, using the attacker's energy to throw that person or apply a neutralizing technique. The key for all this, as Tom teaches it, is to learn how to be centered, with both mind and body relaxed and alert. Tom told us, "Never get in front of a fast-moving train. When someone comes at you in anger, step back and try to figure out where the energy is coming from."

After lunch that day, I met with our president. Fully suited up, I now had the courage to face our issue with his leadership. I told him I wanted to share some concerns of mine about several incidents that had occurred recently. As I started to talk about these incidents, he suddenly exploded. He screamed, "I've had enough of this. You always believe everybody else. I'm not going to take it anymore. I quit!"

That tremendous calm came over me again, even though our president continued to rant and rave. Finally I said to him, "Well, if that's your decision, then good-bye." I calmly walked out of his office. I never got in front of his fast-moving train. When I suited up, I put on God's armor. I then had the strength to step aside instead of getting in the way of his negative energy. I could admit I had made a mistake in hiring this man. I could be at peace even if letting him go risked having people say the One Minute Manager had fallen on his face.

Our former president had some second thoughts the next day and tried to patch things up, but I stood firm. It was clear he just needed to move on.

Again, it would be tempting to say that God solved this personnel problem, that He rewarded me for accepting Him by setting up the meeting with our president and leading the guy to say, "I quit." But I have come to realize that God doesn't work that way. He is not Santa Claus, inviting us to give Him a wish list so He can hand us everything we want. Instead, He promises us something better when we turn our lives over to Him: that He will be with us always, in the good times and the bad.

At Gethsemane, Christ prayed to His Father that He wouldn't have to go through with the agony of the crucifixion, but that prayer was not granted. If God chose not to save His Son, then why should I expect that He would take on the assignment of solving our personnel problem just because Ken Blanchard turned the problem over to Him?

I believe that instead of solving my personnel problem, God opened my eyes when I surrendered to Him. The reward for suiting up was that I discovered I was not alone—that the new suit I was wearing was a suit of armor. After suiting up, I was able to confront the president calmly and reasonably—something I had not been able to do before because I did not think I was up to it. During the meeting, I stood my ground, where before, I might have given in to his demands because I wanted to be loved, to be the good guy. Now I knew I was already loved and no amount of pleasing others would add to that love. The backbone of God's love was the spine that stood the test when the president returned to ask for his job back.

The real story—the true reward for suiting up—is that I was able to take responsibility for cleaning up my own mess, but I didn't have to go into the battle on my own. Maybe the following imaginary conversation with God will show you what I mean. Sheldon Bowles, my good friend and coauthor of *Raving Fans* and *Gung Ho!*, helped me understand this by turning my experience with the president into an imagined conversation with God.

"God, I've got this problem, see, and I need to be sure I'm doing the right thing."

"Okay, Ken, I'm with you. It will feel right. You'll know it's the right way."

"Thanks, God. That's a big help. But . . . well, it's tough. I mean to confront that guy and everything. Lend me Your strength."

"No problem, Ken. I'm with you. No matter what happens, remember you're on My team—and that means I'm on your team."

"That's great, God. But the guy says he's going to quit. I know that feels right. I trust You that it's right. But wow! This guy's anger has really escalated. I'm way out of my comfort zone here. Give me some strength and peace to make the move."

"Still with you, Ken. Confirm he's going. It's your move. Grab the moment. I'll back you all the way no matter what happens."

"I did it, God. He's gone. But now he wants to come back! That's tough. I trusted You that it was the right thing to do, but at the same time, not to give him a second chance. I haven't been perfect either, You know. I'm tempted to let him come back. Give me the courage of my convictions. Give me the strength for this one."

"I'm with you, Ken. I know it hurts. But I'm here all the way. You can do it."

"Thanks, God. You did it. He's gone. Thanks for taking care of him. Thanks for doing it."

"No, Ken. You did it. I was just there to backstop you. To carry you if you fell. I was there to love you even if you failed. Even if you had made more of a mess, Ken, I would still love you. The fact that you handled this problem right does not make Me love you more. You have all of My love already, Ken. All of it."

Suppose I actually made a mistake. The scenario might be something like this.

"God, I trusted my feelings and let him go, but then I learned that he wasn't doing such a bad job after all. The people I trusted had not been telling the truth about him. I've wronged a good man, God. Sorry, God. Sorry I've made a mess of things."

"I'm sorry too, Ken. Learn from it. I can't say I'm pleased that you weren't more careful. But always remember I love you. Even when you're wrong, Blanchard, I love you."

"Glad to hear that, God. I need to know that because now I've got to go and make amends with the man I drove away. I don't know how I'll face him. Give me the strength, Lord. Stand by me."

"I'm here, Ken. You can do it. You won't be alone. I'm coming too. Let's go."

"One last question, God. You said if it felt right to do it that I'd know. Well, it felt right and I did it and I was wrong. What happened, God? Why did You let me down?"

"It's called free will, Ken. I don't get directly involved. If I did, what would be the point of your being alive? Yes, I said to trust your feelings about the decision, but sometimes you aren't honest with yourself. Your ego gets in the way. Or you act too fast without thinking. Sometimes you take the easy way out. Remember, though, right or wrong, I love you. If you were perfect, you'd have My job. You can't always be right, but you can care and learn. Now let's go see that president, Ken. You've got a mighty big One Minute Apology ahead of you and it will be tough. But I know you can do it. I'm going to be with you. I always am."

"Thanks, God. Without You in my corner life would be hell."

"Exactly, Ken. That's it exactly."

Phil Hodges told me one time that to appreciate Christianity and the gift God has given us, you have to recognize the difference between justice, mercy, and grace. With justice, if you commit a crime, you get the penalty you deserve. With mercy, if you commit a crime, you are given less punishment than you deserve. With grace, someone else has already taken the sentence—taken the punishment for you. The Lord loves us so much that He sacrificed His only son, Jesus Christ, to wipe our slate clean and give us the gift of salvation.

That's the story of my journey—how I suited up for the Lord.

Margie Joins the Team

You might be wondering what happened to Margie. Well she suited up a year later after reading Robert Laidlaw's *The Reason Why*, during a ski trip to Aspen with a group of old Cornell friends.

The day before she had hurt her leg skiing, so she decided to take it easy the rest of this trip. Phil Hodges gave Laidlow's little booklet to Margie to read when we all headed off to the slopes.

When I got back to the room at the end of our ski day, Margie said, "Well, I did it!"

I said, "Did what?"

"I suited up," she smiled. "Robert Laidlaw asked for a

decision at the end of *The Reason Why* Hodge gave me, so I bowed my head and did it."

Several years ago Charlie "Tremendous" Jones, author of *Life is Tremendous* and founder of Executive Books, got permission to re-publish *The Reason Why*. Unbeknownst to me he asked Margie to write the forward. I was touched when I read her comments:

*Nearly ten years ago I spent a snowy after-noon reading **The Reason Why** while Ken and friends were skiing. Perhaps like you, I had both noticed and envied the deep joy I saw in people (like Ken) who had taken the promise of forgive-ness of sins and eternal salvation into their hearts by accepting Jesus Christ as their person-al Lord and Savior. It was a mystery to me. How did a person like me come to this decision and take what sounded like a simple but huge step?*

***The Reason Why** is 30 pages long. It very patiently goes through the intellectual questions you and I have about the existence of God, the Bible and the Word of God and, ultimately, God's offer and plan for our salvation and eter-nal life with Him.*

My beliefs, my faith, and my ego were all challenged in this little book as the case for God's wondrous and loving offer was built and rebuilt. At the end I was asked to leave my doubts behind, to rejoice in the invitation by God to take Jesus Christ into my heart as my personal savior, and to accept that offer period.

As I signed and dated this little book, I realized that faith is simply a choice—yes or no. Yes for me has made all the difference.

When Margie told me she had suited up after reading *The Reason Why,* I began to cry. What a great day that was for her and me! You suit up one at a time. Margie is not an emotional decision maker like I am. She is much more thoughtful. She had to suit up on her own timetable. Now we are really on the same team—forever!

DESTINATIONS

*For I know the plans I have for
you," declares the Lord, "plans to
prosper you, and not to harm you,
plans to give you hope and a future.*

Jeremiah 29:11

BRINGING HEAVEN DOWN TO EARTH

I have been traveling on this wonderful earthly spiritual journey now for more than fifteen years. You would think that by now I would have arrived or, at least, be very close to arriving. But arriving implies a specific destination, and to most people the final destination is where we spend eternity. I think that's true but what does that mean for the rest of your life on earth after you suit up for the Lord. Does it lose its importance?

Since grace is a gift and therefore cannot be achieved but only accepted and received through faith, some people think what we do with the rest of our life—our works—is unimportant. Yet that is not true. While faith and belief in Jesus as "the truth and the way" guarantees us a spot in eternity, He was very interested in us becoming disciples, not just believers of the word but also doers of the word. James: 1:22 says it well: "Do not merely listen to the word and so deceive yourselves. Do what it says."

Tony Evans, a great pastor from Dallas, puts this into perspective. He says, "Faith gets you into heaven, but it is your works that bring heaven down to earth." You've probably heard the saying, "he was so heavenly minded that he was no earthly good." It refers to people who focus so much on heaven that they forget about their earthly destinations. I don't want to be like that. I am very interested in bringing "heaven down to earth." What a shame to acknowledge the gift of grace and then go on living as if nothing were different.

When God gets our attention and we accept His grace and forgiveness, our feet are set on a new path. That certainly was true for me. It gave me new priorities and a new way of looking at myself. Although I am still the same person with the same talents He gave me, I now see that I can use those talents to bring glory to His name. And in the process, I am able to become the best person I can be.

Your new destination, then, is really a new vision for your life. Jesse Stoner and I wrote a book entitled *Full Steam Ahead!* about the power of visioning. To us a compelling vision tells you *who you are (your purpose), where you are going (your picture of the future), and what will guide your journey (your values).*

Establishing Your Purpose in Life

What do we mean by your purpose in life? It means your reason for being—something toward which you are always striving. A purpose is different than a goal in that it does not have a beginning or an end—it is ongoing. It gives meaning and definition to our lives.

In *The Power of Ethical Management,* Norman Vincent Peale and I talked about purpose as a particular road you choose to travel. A goal is one of the places you intend to visit on that road. So, while making money is a goal we can strive for, it is not our purpose in life, although some people act like it is and put all their energy into accumulating cash and assets.

Purpose is not about any achievement; it is bigger. It's your *calling*—deciding what kind of business you are in as a person. Having a clear purpose makes it easier to accept God's gift of grace and continue to trust it. After all, if we talk about your calling, we must also talk about the caller. It does not seem reasonable to work on a personal mission statement without dealing with your relationship to the Lord, because they are so interrelated. Acknowledging God's grace sends you off on a journey to wholeness. God already made up the difference between you and 100 with your acceptance of Jesus; now He wants you to be a doer of the word.

So, while we still have the gift of life, our destination as followers of Jesus is to have a clear sense of purpose in serving Him. One of the best ways to do this is to borrow the concept of a mission statement from the business world and develop your own. Have you ever done that?

Richard Bolles, in his essay entitled "How to Find Your Mission in Life," which appears in the appendix of his perennial bestseller *What Color Is Your Parachute?*, helped me a great deal in writing a personal mission statement. He says that everyone's mission statement should include three parts. The first two we share with all humanity and the third is unique to us. The first aspect of your mission statement that is universal is getting to know the Lord better in your life. In other words, it involves growing in your knowledge of the Lord. I think our mission in life starts there.

The second part of everyone's mission statement ought

to include, "making the world a better place to live." Sounds simple, doesn't it? I ask folks at my seminars all the time, "How many of you would like to make the world a better place for your having been here?" All hands go up. Then I ask, "What's your plan?" The room usually goes silent. While everyone would like to make the world better, they usually don't know how to get started.

Bolles has a wonderful strategy. He says you can make the world a better place by the moment-by-moment decisions you make in your interactions with the people with whom you come in contact. He suggests that every time you interact with someone, whether a loved one, a friend, or a person you meet in the street, you have a choice—to add more love to the world or less, more honesty or less, more forgiveness or less, more gratitude or less, or more justice or less.

Suppose you're driving down the highway. Someone on your right is in the wrong lane and obviously needs to get back into your lane. Choice point: Do you add more forgiveness to the world or less? Do you smile and slow down to let that person into your lane, or do you give that person a dirty look (or worse) and step on the gas?

Suppose your spouse yells at you as you're leaving the house. Choice point: Do you add more love to the world or less? Do you go back into the house and give your spouse a hug and say, "I hope your day goes better," or do you yell back and pour fuel on the fire?

I think you get the point. Once you suit up on God's team, your purpose changes from serving yourself to serving others, and your personal mission statement ought to reflect that.

The last part of your mission statement that is unique to you has to do with your *calling*. I've heard of people who suited up and then left successful careers to become ministers or missionaries. I have nothing against that kind of work, but the Bible tells us that everyone in the family of God has a ministry—we do not necessarily have to run a church or move to another country.

God has given you a unique set of gifts. He wired you a certain way. He didn't put you here to keep fighting your weaknesses. That's what my son, Scott, and his coauthor Madeleine Homan argue in their book *Leverage Your Best, Ditch the Rest*. What you love to do is probably what you ought to be doing. So, as you think about your mission statement, ask yourself this question: "What do I love to do?"

Every once in a while I put my arm around a manager who is struggling and tell that person, "You're going to be all right. In fact, you're a beautiful person, but the Lord didn't put you on earth to manage others." Some people often make excellent individual contributors, but they don't have the listening, supporting, or facilitating characteristics to help someone else.

I recognized early in my career that the Lord didn't put me on earth to manage others. Harry Evarts, who retired a number of years ago from a top management position with the American Management Association (AMA), laughs whenever he sees me. My first job out of graduate school was working for him as his administrative assistant when he was dean of the College of Business Administration at Ohio University. We can't decide whether he fired me before I quit or if I quit before he fired me. It probably was a photo finish. At any rate, I was a terrible administrator. With the exception of my executive secretary, Dottie Hamilt, no one in our company reports to me. And since I travel so much, Dottie is not quite sure who she reports to, either. But we've been together for almost ten years, so it all works out.

I got some additional help in writing my mission statement from Tony Robbins, the personal growth guru and bestselling author of *Unlimited Power and Awaken the Giant Within*. During his seminar, "A Date with Destiny," Tony told us to write and rewrite our personal mission statements until we could tell others our mission with real passion and commitment. I wrote: "I am a loving teacher of simple truths who helps and motivates myself and others to awaken to the presence of God in our lives."

When I began to share this with others, I made one change. I added "and example," so that my statement now reads: "I am a loving teacher *and example* of simple truths who helps and motivates myself and others to awaken the presence of God in our lives." Spencer Johnson gave me the new suggested words because he said he knows a lot of people who don't practice what they preach. That certainly includes me from time to time. That's why the pressure to set an example is important.

The reason I made "awaken to the presence of God in

our lives" part of my mission statement is that I feel the biggest addiction we have in the world today is the human E.G.O. In this case, E.G.O. stands for *Edging God Out* and putting ourselves in the center of the universe. When that occurs, we turn our backs on the unconditional love that God offers us and start looking for our self worth in all the wrong places. If I can help myself and others awaken to the presence of God in our lives, we have a better chance to get out of our own way, get to know God better, receive grace, and make the world a better place. I say "we" because I am on the same journey.

What is your mission statement—your reason for being? Think about it. It's important as you attempt to bring heaven down to earth. Why did the Lord put you here?

Creating Your Picture of the Future

The second aspect of a compelling vision is your picture of the future. Where are you going? What would happen if you lived your purpose or mission perfectly every day?

If you're having trouble with that question, you might try an interesting activity that may help you develop a clear picture of the future: Write your own obituary. This gives you a chance—ahead of time—to describe the ideal you. What would you look like? How would you behave? What would you be remembered for? I first got interested in writing my own obituary when I heard a story about Alfred Nobel, the originator of the Nobel Peace Prize. His brother died at the turn of the century and when Alfred got a copy of the newspaper to see what was said about his brother, he was shocked to discover the paper had mixed him up with his brother. So he had the unique opportunity of reading his own obituary over coffee that morning.

When he was younger, Alfred had been involved in the invention of dynamite. What do you think his obituary was all about? Dynamite and destruction.

Nobel was devastated. When he talked with his friends and loved ones about what had happened, they asked, "What is the opposite of destruction? Peace!" So Nobel redesigned his life so he would be remembered for peace.

What would you like to be remembered for? How do you picture your life?

Here's what I would like my obituary to say:

> Ken Blanchard was a loving teacher and example of simple truths whose books and speeches on leadership, management and life helped and motivated himself and others to awaken the presence of God in our lives. He continually challenged and equipped people to live and lead like Jesus. He was a caring child of God, son, brother, spouse, father, grandfather, father-in-law, brother-in-law, godfather, uncle, cousin, friend and colleague who strove to find a balance between success, significance and surrender. He had a spiritual peace about him that permitted him to say "no" in a loving manner to peo-

ple and projects that got him off purpose. He knew full well that *B.U.S.Y.* stood for being under Satan's yoke. He was a person of high energy who was able to see the positive in any event. No matter what happened, he could find a learning or a message in it. Ken Blanchard was someone who trusted God's unconditional love and believed he was the beloved. He felt the most important step he made in life was to suit up for the Lord. He valued integrity, walked his talk, and was a mean and lean 185-pound golfing machine. He will be missed because wherever he went, he made the world a better place for his having been there.

Okay, maybe I got a little carried away with the weight and golfing, but why not? Margie says, "A goal is a dream with a deadline." When you write your obituary before you die, it is a dream—a big-picture goal of what you want your life to be and mean. Once you've suited up, don't hold back. Don't think of your lesser self but your best self, for that is what God intended you to be all along. And don't do it alone. Quiet yourself, pray, and listen to the voice that says, "You are loved."

Determining Your Values

Once you know what your purpose is and you have a clear picture of the future, the third and final aspect of a compelling vision is to determine your *values*—what will guide your journey. I really got to think through my values while I was participating in Tony Robbins' Date With Destiny seminar. I knew values were important, but most of the values work I had done was with organizations. In fact, Michael O'Connor and I wrote a book called *Managing by Values*. And yet, I had never really looked at my own values.

During that enlightening weekend I not only determined what my rank-ordered values should be but also how I would determine whether or not I was living by them. What follows is the product of that important thinking:

I value spiritual peace and know I am living by this value:

- Any time I realize I am a child of God and He loves me no matter what I do.
- Any time I am grateful for my blessings.
- Any time I pray and feel God's unconditional love.

I value love and know I am living by this value:

- Any time I feel loving towards myself and others.
- Any time I am compassionate.
- Any time I feel love in my heart.
- Anytime I feel the love of others.
- Any time my heart fills up with love.
- Any time I look for the love in others.

I value integrity and know I am living by this value:

- Any time I am honest with myself and others.
- Any time I walk my talk.

I value joy and know I am living by this value:

- Any time I let my playful child express itself.
- Any time I wake up feeling grateful for my blessings, the beauty around me and the people in my life.
- Anytime I smile, am happy and laugh and kid.

I value health and know I am living by this value:

- Any time I treat my body with love and respect.
- Any time I exercise.
- Any time I push my body to expand its present limits.
- Any time I eat nutritious food.

I value intelligence and know I am living by this value:

- Any time I do effective evaluation before I act or agree to do something.
- Any time I spend ten minutes to organize my day and ten minutes processing my day.
- Any time I spend two to three hours to organize my week/month.
- Anytime I learn to say, "I choose not to…"
- Anytime I see the impact of a "yes."

Few people have clear written values. But values are important because if you follow them, they will drive your behavior while you are working on your life purpose and picture of the future. When people do have values they often have too many values and/or their values are not rank-ordered. I find that people can't focus on more than three or four values if they really want to impact their behavior. Now you are obviously going to say, "But, Ken, you have six values." Yes, I do, but I also want you to understand that ever since I suited up for the Lord my four guiding values have been *spiritual peace, love, integrity and joy.* I added health and intelligence to the list because those are areas I am working hard on in my life and therefore I wanted to make sure they made my value list. What I probably need to do is make them part of a goal list.

Why should values be rank-ordered? Because life is about value conflicts. When these conflicts arise, people need to know what value they should focus on. When the Pharisees asked Jesus what the greatest commandment was, His answer dealt with both the number of commandments and rank order when He said:

> *Love the Lord your God with all your heart and with all your soul, and with all your mind. This is the first and greatest commandment. And the second is like it: Love your neighbor as yourself. All the law and the prophets hang on these two commandments.*
>
> Matthew 22:37-40

Making My Vision Come Alive

I read my vision statement every day to remind myself of my purpose, my picture of the future and my operating values. I have been doing this since 1992. But it wasn't until 1999, when I co-founded the Center for *FaithWalk* Leadership with Phil Hodges, that this mission took on special meaning in terms of what God really wants me to be focusing my energy on during the rest of my earthly life. I've learned from Henry Blackaby and his *Experiencing God* that our focus in our prayers should not be on God satisfying our needs and helping us accomplish our plans. Instead, the focus should be on Him.

I always smile when I see the saying, "If you want to make God laugh, tell Him your plans." What Blackaby suggests is that we need to watch what God is doing around us and join in. That's when we'll know what our purpose in life is.

According to Blackaby, God is always at work around you. He pursues a continuing love relationship with you that is real and personal. In the process He invites you to become involved with Him in His work. And yet how do you know what His purposes and ways are for you? According to Blackaby God speaks by the Holy Spirit through the Bible, prayer, circumstances—i.e., the people He sends into your life—and the church. God used all of these ways to communicate to me about what I should be doing.

As I said earlier, it started with the circumstance of *The*

One Minute Manager becoming a bestselling book. Part of that success got me invited to be on television and radio programs all over the country. One of the most exciting invitations was to be interviewed by Dr. Robert Schuller on *The Hour of Power,* televised from the Crystal Cathedral.

Dr. Schuller had been very important in my Mom and Dad's life. Ever since he'd started his television ministry, they'd hardly ever missed a Sunday broadcast. When my father died in February 1979 my mom decided to stay out in California for a while. One Sunday in March I said to Mom, "You've never seen Dr. Schuller live, have you?" She said, "No, but I'd love to." I said, "Why don't we go there? His ministry is in Orange County, about an hour and fifteen minutes from our house in San Diego."

So Mom and I headed up to Garden Grove. When we arrived for the service, we found out that this was going to be the last service in the old chapel. Half-way through the service the whole congregation got up and walked into the Crystal Cathedral for the first time. It was absolutely beautiful.

Dr. Schuller's sermon that day was "Every Ending is a New Beginning." My mom turned to me and said with a smile, "See, God knew exactly what I needed to hear today." This was clearly before I had suited up for the Lord, so she wanted to make sure that I understood every important connection with God.

During the service Dr. Schuller interviewed someone. As he was conducting that interview I turned to Mom and said, "Someday I am going to be up there with him." She turned to me and laughed. "How is that going to happen?" I smiled back and said, "I don't know. I just sense it." So it was a real thrill four years later when I was up there with Robert Schuller, with Mom in the congregation.

Dr. Schuller loved *The One Minute Manager* and what he said about it began a process that is continuing to change my life forever. He suggested that Jesus was a classic One Minute Manager. When I asked him to explain why, he was very clear. As I recall the conversation he said, "First, Jesus was very clear on goals, and isn't the first secret of being a One Minute Manager called one-minute goal setting?" I certainly had to agree with that. Then he smiled and said, "Tom Peters didn't invent 'management by wandering around'—Jesus did. He wandered from one village to another, always looking to see if He could catch someone doing something right. When people showed any signs of believing Him and the good news He brought, Jesus would heal them, praise them and encourage them. Isn't the second secret of the One Minute Manager referred to as a One Minute Praising?"

Finally, Dr. Schuller implied that if people were off base, Jesus wasn't afraid to redirect or chastise them as he did with the money lenders in the church. And that was appropriate. "After all, the final secret of the One Minute Manager is the one minute reprimand."

Robert Schuller's comments about Jesus as a One Minute Manager got me thinking. As I began to deepen in my faith, delve into the Bible, pray and attend church, I quickly realized that everything I had ever taught or written about, Jesus did. And He did it perfectly with twelve inexperienced people. After studying leadership for more than thirty years, I came to the conclusion that Jesus is the greatest leadership role model of all time. And do we ever need a different leadership role model today!

Today in the headlines we read about corporate American leaders who exploit privileges of position bringing ruin to employees and investors. Meanwhile, citizens of underdeveloped countries languish in poverty and hopelessness in a leadership vacuum. At the same time all across the country, the witness and ministry of a number of churches have been compromised and stymied by a crisis of integrity in their leaders. In stark contrast to these failures and foibles of twenty-first century leadership stands the perfect leadership role model, Jesus of Nazareth.

As a result of this insight and the realization that few, if any, divinity schools or pastors were teaching about Jesus as a great leadership role model, in 1999 I co-founded with Phil Hodges the Center for *FaithWalk* Leadership. The initial intent of the Center was to help people walk their faith in the marketplace. The Center was started after Phil and I began working on *Leadership by the Book* with Bill Hybels.

When we started the Center we began training people to be servant leaders as Jesus had mandated. We are convinced that Jesus calls all who follow Him to become His leadership disciples. He was very clear and emphatic in

His instructions that His followers were to be like servants when John and James seemed to be vying for a special leadership role among the disciples.

> *Jesus called them together and said, "You know that the rulers of the Gentiles lord it over them, and their high officials exercise authority over them. Not so with you. Instead, whoever wants to become great among you must be your servant, and whoever wants to be first must be your slave—just as the Son of Man did not come to be served, but to serve and to give His life as a ransom for many."*
>
> Matthew 20:25-28

The key phrase is "not so with you." That Jesus called us to a way of leading born out of service and obedience is clear and unequivocal. No plan B is implied or offered. No restrictions or limitations to only religious leadership are made or inferred. For Christian leaders this is not a suggestion, it is a mandate.

Today—with the help of Greg Bunch, a member of the Center's national board, and folks he works with at Brand Trust in Chicago—the Center for *FaithWalk* Leadership is an address at best. They helped us to realize that our purpose is to inspire and equip people to lead like Jesus. We are in the LEAD LIKE JESUS business. We now call our ministry a movement because our hope is that someday, everyone everywhere will know someone who truly leads like Jesus. We imagine a world in which leaders serve rather than rule, a world in which they give rather than take. We imagine leaders who seek to produce results and services. We recognize this only happens as leaders adopt Jesus as their leadership role model and grow in His likeness.

Our vision for the future is:

- Jesus adopted as the role model of all leaders.
- All Christian churches led by Jesus-like leaders.
- Every Christian taught to *lead like Jesus.*
- Non-Christians are drawn to Jesus by the practicality and positive effects of Christians who *lead like Jesus.*

If that is our vision, what will guide our journey?

Our values are to:

- Honor God in everything we do.
- Build relationships built on trust and respect.
- Maintain integrity and excellence in programs and services.
- Practice stewardship.

Since I am not retiring but re-firing, my goal is to take the message of Lead Like Jesus all over the world. Annually we are doing Lead Like Jesus Celebration simulcasts all over the country and will soon be moving around the world. People who hear about us can go to our

LeadLikeJesus.com website and learn what a fabulous boss I am working for now.

My faith has also impacted my work at our training and consulting company. I changed my title from Chairman to Chief Spiritual Officer: CSO. That title better describes my role as energizer, cheerleader, and supporter of our company's vision and values. Every day I leave a voice mail message for everyone in our company–some 300 people–in which I do three things. First, people tell me who we should pray for. When family members, friends, or one of our associates is hurting, I let people know so they can send prayers and positive energy their way. Second, I praise people. Folks in our company tell me who are unsung heroes, so I can recognize their efforts. Finally, I leave an inspirational message around our vision and values. Since we are in the business of helping individuals and organizations to lead at a higher level, that has been an exciting way for me to enter my day and focus and motivate our people.

Now you know not only my final destination—where I get to go because of my faith—but also my earthly destination—how I want to bring heaven to earth. The question now is: How do I stay on course?

STAYING ON COURSE

*Blessed is the man who perseveres under trial,
because when he has stood the test he will receive
the crown of life that God has promised
to those who love Him.*

James 1:12

At the end of my seminars, people often come up to me and say, "Ken, I'm committed to being a One Minute Manager. I'm committed to being the kind of manager you described today."

My response is quick: "I'm not concerned about your commitment. But I am concerned about your commitment to your commitment." People say diets don't work. Diets work fine. People don't work. They keep on breaking their commitment to their commitment.

I have had that same question about myself: Would I keep my commitment to the Lord? Would I continue to believe in His unconditional love? Would I continue to trust my life to Him and see what happens? Would I go back to living life with myself as the center when the glow of my faith wore off? Would I forget about my relationship with the Father and resume thinking that I can figure everything out by myself?

Bill Hybels put this in perspective for me when he said, "God already knows we can't keep our commitment, yet He still loves us." What impact does this have on my present life?

My energy is focused on how I stay on course today, be the kind of person I want to be, and please God.

As Hybels suggests, the key to staying on course is realizing my present is secure in the unconditional love that God has given me through the grace of His son. That's so hard for us to understand, because as human beings, we have difficulty giving up control and believing that it is *already done*. We're led astray by voices in our heads that try to convince us there are still things we must do to deserve the Lord's unconditional love. Boy, would I like a chance to undo some of the things I've done over the years that are inconsistent with who I want to be in the world.

Jesus Himself faced those same temptations. The inspirational writer Henri Nouwen relates in a humorous and powerful way how Jesus responded to the temptations of the Evil One who said, "Prove that you are beloved. Do something! Change these stones into bread. Be sure that you are famous. Jump from the temple and you will be on TV and grab some power so you will have real influence. Don't you want some influence? Is that not what you came for?"

Jesus said, "No! I don't have to prove anything. *I am already the beloved.*"

Why is it that so often we get distracted and off course? Is it because we don't believe that we are the beloved and that the same voice that was talking to Jesus is also talking to us? What's keeping me—and others who have already acknowledged grace—from trusting God totally and bringing Him into our daily concerns and decisions? I think it's because we want to feel valuable, worthy, important. The irony is that we are valued and loved by God without doing anything to merit it. All we need to do is receive and accept; to open our hearts and minds to the love that awaits us all.

Why don't we do that? Because the Lord gave us free will and with it came a choice to accept His love or not.

With free will we have the capacity to make our lives happy or make them miserable.

H.E.L.P. for the Journey

Given the fact that I am not a robot and have the freedom to choose which direction I turn, how do I keep myself on course and live according to my vision? How do I get back on course if I stray?

I have learned to seek H.E.L.P., an acronym that stands for *H*umility, *E*xcellence, *L*istening, and *P*raising. I have found it is a useful framework for helping me remember to trust the Lord and His unconditional love for me. Let me share this H.E.L.P. formula with you in more detail.

Humility. "People with humility don't think less of themselves, they just think of themselves less." In that quote from our book *The Power of Ethical Management,* Norman Vincent Peale and I were suggesting that it's healthy to feel good about yourself—but don't get carried away. The problem is with the ego.

As I said earlier, E.G.O. stands for *E*dging *G*od *O*ut. When we start to get a distorted image of our own importance and see ourselves as the center of the universe, we lose touch with who we really are as children of God. Our thinking blurs, and we lose the sense of our connection with home base, others, and our true selves. Like the little girl trying to talk with her baby brother, we forget what God is like.

There are two types of ego-centeredness: self-doubt

and false pride. Both are enemies of humility. People with self-doubt are consumed with their shortcomings and tend to be hard on themselves. People with false pride think they don't need grace and are out of touch with their own vulnerability and the fact that they fall short of 100. Both have a hard time believing that they are loved.

I have to confess that self-doubt is an area that can easily shove me off course. As a people person, I don't want anyone to disapprove of me. When I read the evaluation comments from my seminar participants or from the readers of my books, even though the overwhelming majority are positive, I tend to focus on the negative ones. It's difficult for me to accept praise. After a successful seminar or speech, I will catch myself saying things like, "It was no big deal." Those words may sound appropriately humble, but they are just my way of avoiding listening to positive feedback. Also, in our company I have had trouble making hard personnel decisions (as you learned earlier) because I'm uncomfortable when people get upset with me.

It's difficult for people with self-doubt to acknowledge grace. They think they don't deserve it. They fail to realize that God did not make junk. To keep self-doubt from convincing you that you have to achieve God's love, remember that you were made by some pretty good hands. *You are the beloved.*

People with false pride have trouble believing in God, much less accepting Jesus as their Savior. They are unwilling to see their own errors or any difficulties in themselves. The story of Adam and Eve is the story of false pride. The serpent didn't offer them an apple because he thought they wanted some fruit. He played on their egos, telling Eve, "Your eyes will be opened and you will be like God" if she would just taste the forbidden fruit.

When our false pride gets in the way, we think we are like God. We lose touch with the fact that we all fall short of 100. We think we deserve all the credit, that we're the source of all good ideas, that our work is the most important, that we don't need the help of others.

It's easy to understand that self-doubt comes from lack of self-esteem, because people afflicted with it on a daily basis act as if they are worth less than others. It is less obvious with people who have false pride, because they behave as if they are worth more than others. People with false pride—those who act as if they are the only ones who count—are really trying to make up for their own lack of self-esteem. They overcompensate for their "not okay" feelings by trying to control everything and everybody around them. In the process, they make themselves unlovable to everyone who comes in contact with them.

Over the years I've found myself occasionally entangled in some very unpleasant legal hassles with former colleagues. None of the disputes should have gotten to the point where legal involvement was needed. But I was convinced I was right and they felt they were right. In the process of trying to be right, we all forgot that *we are the beloved*. As a result, in many ways we all lost. Pride clouds our vision. We don't see things clearly, and we have a particularly hard time seeing the other person's point of view. When we suit up and trust God, His love helps heal the blind spots.

So why did these legal hassles come along, even though I had put my trust in God? Shouldn't Christians have easier lives? That's old naive thinking that falsely tells us that if we love God, then everything will go right for us. When we think this way, we get angry when trouble comes our way, and we are tempted to go back to doing things on our own. After all, God let us down.

I have come to learn that when bad things happen, that is the time to learn and grow. In my case, the financial and emotional drain of legal hassles has had a purpose. The Bible says that all quarrels are the result of pride. The Lord needed to knock me over the head so that I could relearn (hopefully for good) that being right is the most useless of human endeavors. The worst thing about having to be right is that you have to find someone to be wrong. That's completely counter to the good news of Christianity and its focus on love. Henri Nouwen again gives us guidance:

> And in the spirit of God the fact that you are chosen and blessed and beloved does not mean that others are less so. In fact, the opposite is happening when you discover your belovedness. You have an inner eye that allows you to see the belovedness of other people and call that forth. That's the incredible mystery of God's love. The more you know how deeply you are loved, the

more you'll see how deeply your sisters and brothers in the human family are loved.

In Gordon MacDonald's book *Ordering Your Private World,* he makes an important distinction between driven and called people. People who are *driven* think they own everything—their job, their possessions, their spouses, their kids, and their ideas. As a result, they spend all their time trying to protect what they own. *Driven* people are constantly calling in the lawyers to set matters right.

On the other hand, people who are *called* think everything is on loan from God. Since they don't own anything, they figure their role in life is to shepherd everybody and everything that comes their way. In relationships, it means helping to bring the best out in others. Being helpful is more important than being right. Instead of calling in the lawyers, *called* people are constantly looking to God to set things right.

It's interesting for me to see how self-doubt and false pride play out in managers. When they are addicted to either ego infliction, it erodes their effectiveness.

Managers dominated with self-doubt are often called do-nothing bosses. They are described as never around, always avoiding conflict, and not very helpful. They often leave people alone even when they are insecure and don't know what they are doing. They don't seem to believe in themselves or trust in their own judgment. They value others' thoughts more than their own—especially the thoughts of those they report to. As a result, they rarely speak out and support their own people. Under pressure they seem to defer to whomever has the most power.

At the other end of the spectrum are the controllers. These are managers dominated by false pride. Even when they don't know what they are doing, they have a high need for power and control. Even when it's clear to everyone that they are wrong, they keep on insisting they are right. These folks aren't much for supporting their people, either. If everyone is upbeat and confident, the controller throws out the wet blanket. They support their bosses over their people because they want to climb the hierarchy and be part of the bosses' crowd.

If any of this sounds a bit too close for comfort, don't be alarmed. Most of us have traces of both self-doubt and false pride, because the issue is really ego. We are stuck, all alone, focusing only on ourselves. The good news of the gospel is that results or approval from others is no longer important. "Done" means just that. Jesus took care of it. If we can accept God's unconditional love, we set the stage for receiving His grace. And when you receive it, your slate is wiped clean. When you realize that God is in your corner, you also know you have all the support, love, and backing you'll ever need. It's a humbling experience. Norman Vincent Peale once told me that bowing your head and admitting you can't save yourself is the toughest test of self-esteem. But until we get out of our own way and start believing that *we are the beloved,* we'll continue to avoid suiting up and trusting our lives to the Lord. We will be *driven* and not *called.*

The minute you begin to think you can gain points with God by doing great things, you are straying off course. Humility brings you back. Jim Collins certainly learned that from his study of leadership reported in his book *Good to Great*. He found two characteristics to describe great leaders: *will* and *humility*. Will is the determination to follow through on a vision/mission/goal. Humility is the capacity to realize that leadership is not about the leader, it is about the people and what they need.

According to Collins, when things are going well for typical self-serving leaders, they look in the mirror, beat their chests, and tell themselves how good they are. When things go wrong, they look out the window and blame everyone else. On the other hand, when things go well for great leaders, they look out the window and give everybody else the credit. When things go wrong, these servant leaders look in the mirror and ask questions like: "What could I have done differently that would have allowed these people to be as great as they could be?" That requires real humility. That is a requirement if I want to lead like Jesus.

Excellence. Most people think of excellence as being the best—better than anyone else. Unfortunately, there can only be one Number One. To think of excellence in this manner forces you to do those things that ultimately pull you away from God. It sets life up in a win-lose proposition where the only person that matters to you is good old Number One. But the kind of excellence that helps keep you on course is available to everyone. It's the process of rising up to the Lord's standard of excellence for you, which is nothing more and nothing less than your becoming the very best you that you can be.

A number of years ago I spent a week with Rabbi Harold Kushner, the author of the bestselling book *When Bad Things Happen to Good People*. We were at a YPO University in Acapulco, and his presentation there was about a follow-up book, *When All You've Ever Wanted Is Not Enough*. From Rabbi Kushner I relearned that there are two acts in life: achieve and connect.

Act 1—achieve—is a natural act for human beings. After all, we are one of the only animals that can have goals outside of physical survival. Much of life for human beings today consists of not just looking for and accumulating food or overcoming dangers to security but also building and creating. Every freeway around a city on Monday morning is choked with thousands of people who are fulfilling their achieve acts. The problem is that many people think that it's the only act in town. As a result, right up to their last breath these people are making life revolve around the next sale, the next triumph, the next victory. One of the hardest lessons for us to learn is that the person who dies with the most toys does not win.

There is nothing wrong with achieving, for God put within us a desire to better ourselves and the world around us. The problems come when we put too much emphasis on achieving.

Richard N. Bolles spoke to this in an interview entitled "Loving God and Loving Our Careers":

If you show me someone who is enraptured by his or her work but has no religious convictions, I would be extremely pessimistic about trying to talk that individual out of basing his or her self-esteem too much on work performance. Unless a real crisis occurs in that person's life, and he or she becomes open, chances are there will be no change. That kind of absorption with one's career is almost like a drug. It's not just the job that strokes one's ego, it's the whole context of the work—fame, wealth, prestige, etc.—that reinforce over-dependency on one's professional identity.

Rabbi Kushner says that in all his years as a rabbi he's never heard anyone say on his deathbed, "I wish I had gone to the office more." Instead, what do they wish? That they'd loved more, spent more time with family, friends, and loved ones. Most people never get beyond Act 1 in their lives.

Act 2—connect—is about relationships, the most important of which is your relationship to God. In Act 2, you realize it is important to connect with the Lord, with others, and with your own true self. Unfortunately, in our society few people think about Act 2 until they've had a midlife crisis or a near-death experience. When tragedy strikes, they begin to raise questions about what life is really about, what it means. While it is never too late to open the curtain on Act 2, think of all you miss by waiting until something bad happens.

People who successfully move on to Act 2 are more likely to stay on course in their relationship to God. They also have a better chance of moving on to an integration of and a balance between achieving and connecting. Let's call that Act 3. When you define who you are by what it says on your business card, there isn't much, if any, room in your life for Act 2, and without Act 2, you can't go on to Act 3. An overemphasis on achievement makes it difficult to acknowledge grace, because any thought about salvation or entry into heaven becomes another achievement. That leads to the "do" approach to religion, which leads to people dropping out because, in the end, you can never do enough.

Acknowledging grace requires that you accept that it is "done." You do not have to do anything more, because you cannot earn your way into acceptance. You are already accepted. *You are already the beloved.* So now you can forget about trying to gain something for the sake of achievement and begin working at becoming the best person God intended you to be.

I love the story that Vernon Howard relates in his book, *The Mystic Path to Cosmic Power*:

> A prince was kidnapped at birth from his father's palace. Raised in poverty in a wretched village, he rebelled against the poverty of his life. He constructed careful

plans for becoming king of the land. Through a series of schemes and battles, he won the throne. But he was anxious, hostile. Having taken the kingdom by force, he lived in dreaded fear of other ambitious men. It was day-to-day misery.

Then he learned his true identity. He is a king by birthright. He sees the folly of trying to regain by force what is already his inheritance. Now, with his kingly consciousness, there is no fear, no threat, only quiet dominion.

Every one of us is a king or queen if we will only believe that *we are the beloved*. We don't need to be anything or anybody—we already are somebody. And no one can steal your throne from you with schemes or battles. It is yours as long as you want it.

In recent years I ask people in my management seminars, "How many of you have children?" Many hands go up. Then I ask, "How many of you love your children?" They laugh as the same hands go up. Then I raise the key question: "For how many of you is your love of your children dependent upon their achievements? If they are successful, you will love them. If they aren't, you won't." Not one hand ever goes up. "So love of your children does not depend on what they achieve or how much power or influence they gain," I continue. "And yet, why won't you and I accept that kind of unconditional love from our Father?"

Only when we do, according to Henri Nouwen, can we begin to hear our Father's comforting words:

I hold you safe under My wings.
You can come home always to Me
whose name is Compassion!
Whose name is Love!

If you keep that image in mind—"that's where I belong"—you can live in the middle of this world and deal with enormous amounts of success as well as enormous amounts of failure without losing your identity. Because your identity is that *you are the beloved.*

I need a constant reminder that I am already loved or I can get caught in Act 1 like everyone else. After *The One Minute Manager* became successful, I then came out with *Putting the One Minute Manager to Work,* then *Leadership and the One Minute Manager,* then *The One Minute Manager Gets Fit,* and so on.

A friend of mine, Red Scott, brought me back down to earth when he said, "Blanchard, you caught lightning in the glass with *The One Minute Manager.* Enjoy it or you will spend the rest of your life trying to catch it again." So now, even though I still write a lot of books, I am not anxiously checking the bestseller list every month. I am more concerned about the potential impact on those who have read one of my books. I love the story about the man walking down the beach one day who sees a young boy busy picking up starfish that have been washed up on the beach and throwing them back in the ocean. The man stops and asks the youngster why he is doing that. He says, "If I don't they will die."

Looking around, the man says to the boy, "But son, there are thousands of starfish on the beach. How can you make a difference?"

The young boy bends over, picks up a starfish and throws it back in the water. Then he smiles and says, "I bet I made a difference to that one."

We can all make a difference where we are planted.

If we can begin to accept unconditional love from our Father, we no longer have to focus on being out there with results, accumulation, power, acceptance, control, or other earthly things. Now we can focus on our own sense of personal excellence and the journey—how to live our lives. We can begin to live according to God's law.

Does this mean that achievement is bad? Absolutely not. Just don't focus on it as your reason for being. Amrit Desai says it well in John Scherer's wonderful little book *Work and the Human Spirit:* "The world is full of ego-giants who have found great success and great misery at the same time. There has never been a shortage of miserably rich, miserably successful people."

The emptiness and misery goes away when you have an inner peace that comes from accepting God's love and receiving His gift of grace. Your focus shifts from excelling in the eyes of others to excelling in the eyes of God. And the great irony is that when you acknowledge God's grace in your life, you get results—only now they come easier, and not by some sort of supernatural miracle in which God removes every barrier from your life. Think about it. Once you break out of the achievement game, you are free to do those things that you really like and to do for the right reasons.

Larry Moody, director of Search Ministries, is a friend of mine. Besides helping business leaders with their walk with the Lord, Larry helped start a Wednesday night Bible study on the PGA golf tour. He's a marvelous preacher who has made a real difference in the lives of his golfing congregation, which includes, among others, Paul Azinger, Bernard Langer, Tom Lehman, Larry Mize, Larry Nelson, Corey Pavin, Scott Simpson and the late Payne Stewart.

Larry and his colleagues teach the meaning of grace to these players week after week. They emphasize that whether they win or lose that week they are still loved. They can't win enough tournaments to get any more love or salvation. Given that, they might as well go out and play well since there is no "real" pressure.

When who you are doesn't depend on your achievements and acceptance by others, does that make a difference? You bet! Margie and I witnessed that during the 1993 Masters. It so happened that the last day of the tournament fell on Easter Sunday. Beginning that day, Bernard Langer was leading the tournament. There's tremendous pressure on the leader of any tournament, much less the prestigious Masters.

Most golfers say it's much easier to be the challenger

than the leader on the last day. When a leader loses, every-one talks about why that person choked. It took Nick Faldo years to overcome being called "Foldo" because he blew a number of tournaments. Lost tournaments also haunted Greg Norman's career.

It was fun watching Langer on this special Sunday. He seemed to be what Chuck Hogan calls "mentally alert but physically relaxed." He seemed to be enjoying himself. When the smart decision would seem to be to play it safe (like his second shot on the famous par 5 thirteenth), he would go for it. He won the tournament by four strokes.

During the traditional interview of the winner by the president of Augusta National Golf Club, a comment was made about this being one of the greatest days of Bernard Langer's life. While Langer admitted winning the Masters was important, what was really special to him was "win-ning it on the anniversary of the resurrection of my Lord."

I'll never forget the comment Tom Landry, the leg-endary Dallas Cowboys coach, made when he was asked how he was able to remain so calm on the field no matter what happened: "It's easy because I have my priorities in order. First comes my Lord, second comes my wife, then comes my kids, and finally my job. If I lose on Sunday, I have a lot left over."

That hit me like a thunderbolt; I knew it was not true with most people, including myself at times. So many of us think life is all about winning. But I like the words of the late tennis star Arthur Ashe: "True heroism is remark-ably sober, very undramatic. It's not the urge to surpass all others at whatever cost, but the urge to serve others at whatever cost."

Am I suggesting that if you acknowledge God's grace in your life you'll be a star athlete or winning football coach? Not at all. But as these men each shared in their own way, putting God first takes the pressure to perform off your shoulders, and most of the time, that allows us to be the best person God intended us to be. That's the kind of excellence that keeps us on course.

I am a golf fanatic. I love the game. In recent years, I have started to play much more N.A.T.O. golf. N.A.T.O. stands for Not Attached To Outcome. When I play N.A.T.O. golf I usually play much better. Why? Because I am not my score. When I am not attached to outcome I can get myself into the rhythm and the joy of the game. As a result, in recent years, I never met a golf game I didn't like.

I had the privilege of writing *Everyone's a Coach* with Don Shula, legendary coach of the Miami Dolphins and the winningest coach in NFL history. Don's favorite saying during his coaching year was "Success is not forever and failure isn't fatal." He felt strongly that you can't afford to be overconfident in victory or be consumed by failure. When Don was coaching he went to Mass every morning he possibly could to give thanks and ask for help. While he wanted to win—and there was nobody more competitive than he was—his faith kept winning and losing in perspective. For more than thirty years Don not only won a minimum of ten games a season, but he kept the Lord and his family at the top of his priorities.

Whenever you're tempted to veer off course and try to make a name for yourself, remember that if you go it alone you're bound to get caught in the achievement game—a game you can never win. Focus instead on becoming excellent in God's eyes and enjoy the blessings that follow.

Listening. One of my teachers used to say: "If God had wanted us to talk more than listen, He would have given us two mouths." One reason we have trouble staying on course and trusting God's grace is that we don't take time to quiet ourselves and listen to the Lord. We are undisciplined in inner listening. Henri Nouwen suggests that in spiritual terms, discipline is creating some space for God—space where God can act, speak, and let something happen that surprises us and lets us know He is there. This means that we have to stop filling up all our time or being preoccupied in the time we have alone.

Why is solitude so hard for us? In our collaboration, Norman Vincent Peale and I realized that we all have two selves: an inner self that is thoughtful, reflective, and a good listener; and an outer, task-oriented self that is focused on achieving and often too busy to learn. The latter self is what drives us in Act 1, the act of achieving. The attention of the inner self is on Act 2 and Act 3—connecting with people and finding significance in life. It is the vehicle we have that helps us listen to the Lord—the caller—and makes sure we are living according to God's purpose for us.

The problem is that it takes longer to awaken our inner self in the morning. When the alarm (isn't that an awful term?) goes off, most of us leap out of bed into our task-oriented selves without giving our inner selves a thought. We eat while we wash and then we're off to our first meeting or activity of the day. We race around from one thing to another, with lunch and dinner squeezed in somewhere. At the end of the day, we fall exhausted into bed with hardly enough energy to say good night to the loved one lying next to us. The next day is more of the same. Pretty soon, one day leads into another, and life becomes little more than a blur.

It becomes a rat race. As Lily Tomlin said, "The trouble with being in a rat race is that even if you win the race, you're still a rat."

The way to avoid the rat race and stay on course is to honor the inner self by seeking solitude—times when we can be "alone with God, and God alone."

Why is solitude so important in keeping you on your journey? Henri Nouwen says it well:

> Because it's the place where you can listen to the voice of the One who calls you the beloved. That's what prayer is all about. To pray is to listen to the voice of the One who calls you my beloved daughter, my beloved son, my beloved child. To pray is to let that

voice speak to the center of your being—to your guts. And let that voice resonate in your whole being. Who am I? *I am the beloved.*

How can you find time for solitude? I recommend you enter your day more slowly. People have talked about quiet time with the Lord in the morning for years, whether it be called "the morning watch" or special time for "personal devotions." Let me share what has worked for me, although I confess that it takes discipline. I must admit I don't do what I describe every day. It's stupid but true. It's good old free will in action again. My hunch is that all of us have the same problem—we know we need to spend more time in quiet reflection, but we let other things crowd that time. Maybe that's why mornings work best for me. When I am being really good to myself, I try to make quiet time the first priority of the day before anything else—like a phone call—has a chance to interfere.

When my day starts off well, one of the first things I do is sit quietly and relax. After some deep breathing, I begin doing some stretching to help rehabilitate a couple of nagging injuries to my left hip and knee. I mention stretching because while I'm on my back working on my flexibility, it's a perfect time to pray and listen. I start my prayers with a Psalm:

This is the day the Lord hath made.
Let us rejoice and be glad in it.
Psalm 118:24

From Bob Buford, I learned to pray in four areas depicted by the acronym ACTS:

Adoration: This is where all prayers should begin—telling the Lord that you love Him and appreciate all He has done and created.

> *Yours, O Lord,*
> *is the greatness and power*
> *and the glory and the majesty*
> *and the splendor,*
> *for everything in heaven and earth is yours.*
> *Yours, O Lord, is the kingdom;*
> *You are exalted as head over all.*
>
> I Chronicles 29:11

Confession: Since we still fall short of God's perfection, we need to make sure that we are cleansed of every sin we have committed.

> *If we confess our sins,*
> *He is faithful and just*
> *and will forgive us our sins,*
> *and purify us from all unrighteousness.*
>
> I John 1:9

Thanksgiving: I think one of the reasons Thanksgiving Day is such a treasured holiday is that we truly enjoy being thankful. So why not do it every day? During this part of my prayer, I thank God specifically for all that He has done for me since the last time we talked.

Sing and make music in your heart
to the Lord,
always giving thanks to God the Father
for everything, in the name
of our Lord Jesus Christ.

Ephesians 5:19–20

Supplication: This is just another word for asking for what you need. I like to start with prayers for others and then ask for my own needs to be met. I have a big wish list. My biggest wish is to give myself and the people I love the strength to proclaim, "Not what I want, but *Thy* will be done, on earth as it is in heaven." According to God's Word, we can ask with confidence:

Ask and it will be given to you;
seek and you will find;
knock and the door will be
opened to you.

Matthew 7:7

Bill Hybels suggested I write my prayers down because I would be amazed at how many come true. When I do that in a journal, it helps me remember my blessings and how much the Lord listens.

During my prayer time, I always spend a few moments in silence, listening. Now you may have heard a preacher say, "God told me…" and wondered what he was talking about. He gives the impression that God speaks to him directly in a clear, loud voice. I admit that I have not been on this journey long enough to know all the answers, but I have to confess I have never heard God speak in an audible voice. Yet, I'd also have to say I am convinced I have heard from God. Usually, it's through people He puts in my path. Whenever I meet an interesting person I always think to myself, *God, what do You want me to learn?* When I am quiet before Him and ask questions like that, my thoughts are directed to those things He wants me to think about or do. That's when it is particularly important to listen.

God also speaks through His Word, the Bible. Keith Jackson, who was the All-Pro tight end with the Miami Dolphins when I was writing with Don Shula, told his teammates that the Bible stands for, "*B*asic *I*nstruction *B*efore *L*eaving *E*arth." That's a humorous way to remember that God inspired writers to preserve His teachings so that we would know how to live. Spending time each day reading the Bible gives you direct access to God. It is more than a reading assignment; it is a way to understand how God wants you to live. I seldom come away from reading the Bible without learning some important new nugget of truth about my journey.

Listening, for me, also includes reading other helpful devotional books. In addition to reading the Bible each morning, I usually read a selection from a daily devotional—a collection of inspirational readings designed to be read through in a year. My perennial favorite is *The Daily Word* (a monthly publication my mother first gave me when I was a child), but there are many wonderful inspirational books on the market.

On an ideal day, when I am finished praying and reading, I end my time of solitude before God by doing some exercise. A lot of people exercise for their physical health, not realizing that it's also good for their spiritual health as well. As one who believes God made me, I think it is important to take care of my body even though I often don't act that way. The Bible calls the body the "temple of the Lord," and I need to be good to this old temple. But I also know that during my daily walk I can continue listening to God.

Here again, we need to be careful about treating exercise as another achievement. Some people turn running or biking or some other good form of activity into their own religion. They measure their performances and get down on themselves when they don't measure up.

A dear friend of mine, Jim Ballad, with whom I co-authored *Whale Done!: The Power of Positive Relationships*, was a morning jogger for more than twenty years. (He's now more of a walker.) I loved to be around Jim when people asked him how far he ran every day. His reply was, "I don't know."

They'd usually counter with, "Well, how long do you jog each day?"

Again, Jim would say, "I don't know. My jogging is not about getting anywhere. It's just the way I choose to enter my day."

What a great approach to exercise. And what a great way to listen. A morning walk helps keep me on course on my journey.

When fog settles in over a seaport, ships listen for the foghorn to know where the dangers are. The sound of the horn helps them stay on course. We, too, need to listen so that we don't stray off course. The old habit of charging hard through life leaves little time for talking to Him and listening to His reply.

Praising. Spencer Johnson and I emphasized in *The One Minute Manager* that the key to developing people is to catch them doing something right so you can pat them on the back and recognize their performance. Nothing motivates people more than being caught in the act of doing something right. If you are to stay on course in your walk with God, you need to begin to do the same thing with yourself.

When was the last time you caught yourself doing something right? Unless you're unusual, you find it hard to praise yourself. Most of the time, you catch yourself doing things wrong and then feel bad about it. No wonder we have a hard time feeling as if *we are the beloved.*

Recognizing the difficulty of receiving praise, Margie and I went out of our way to teach our kids, Scott and Debbie, to become comfortable with receiving compliments as they were growing up. In fact, we taught them to follow a word of praise with the affirmation, "Thanks for noticing." I'll never forget the time friends arrived for a visit one day before Margie and I had gotten home from work. Scott, who was a teenager at the time, was there to greet them. He showed them to their room, got them something to drink, and generally entertained them. When we got home, they praised Scott for his hospitality in front of us. He said, "Thanks for noticing. It's important to me that Mom and Dad's friends and my friends feel at home here." Is it any wonder that Scott ended up going to the Hotel School at Cornell and studying the hospitality industry and now works with us as Director of Client Services. Cheering him on throughout the writing of his bestselling book, *Leverage Your Best, Ditch the Rest* with Madeleine Homan, has been a real joy. In case you are wondering about Debbie, she went to the University of Colorado, studied communications and is heading up our Sales operation.

When it comes to catching yourself doing things right, praising is all about self-talk. A number of years ago I co-founded the Golf University in San Diego with a top teaching professional. The reason I got involved in such a venture is that not only am I a golf fanatic, but I also think golf is the closest to life of any sport. In fact, I say golf stands for *G*ame *O*f *L*ife *F*irst.

In most sports, you are reacting to someone else. If that person is bigger, faster, stronger, or better than you are, it's hard for you to compete. In golf, you don't react to anyone else. That little white ball sits there and waits for you to hit it. And sometimes in golf you are hitting it better than you should and you have to deal with success. At other times, you hit it worse than you should and must deal with failure. In golf, as in life, you get good breaks and bad ones you don't deserve as well as ones you do deserve—and you must deal with all of this in four and a half hours. I can learn more about someone in one round of golf than working with them for a long period of time. Golf brings out the best and worst in people.

When we conduct one of our Golf University classes, we not only teach people the mechanical part of the game—how to hit the golf ball in different situations—but also the mental side. On the mental side of things we focus on self-talk, because that part of the game is usually negative for most players. Most golfers beat themselves up on the golf course. I played with a fellow once who yelled at himself, "You idiot! How can you be so stupid?" almost before he hit the ball. No matter how he shot, it wasn't good enough. I suggested he quit the game since it seemed to cause him such grief. My fear is that he lives his life the same way—always finding fault with himself.

If you're going to stay on course in your journey, you need to focus on catching yourself doing something right. How do you get started? Bill Hybels gave me a marvelous suggestion in his book *Honest to God?* For a long time people had told him he should keep a journal. But being competitive, he was always sidetracked by trying to think how he could write a better journal than anyone else. And, after all, he knew people who wrote in their journals in four colors. Others wrote poems and the like in their journals. So he never got around to keeping a journal because he knew it would never be the best. Then he became the chaplain for the Chicago Bears when all-pro linebacker Mike Singletary, a devout Christian and member of his church, was on the team

Every Monday morning he would conduct a Bible study for some of the players and staff. After the Bible study the team always watched the films from the weekend game. They would watch for things they did well and could feel good about as well as the things they did poorly and needed to improve upon. One day when Bill was heading back to his church, it hit him like a thunderbolt. *That's it!* he thought. *That's how to write a journal.*

His thought was to write the word "Yesterday" at the top of the page and then relive the day before in terms of things he did or thought that he felt good about and the things he would like to live over. Now his journal was unique to him, and he would be able to keep his ego from letting his journal be a competitive game.

Keeping a journal that monitors yesterday's triumphs sets you up for self-praise. When I do my "yesterday" journal, I start by catching myself doing things right. What did I do yesterday that makes me proud? What did I do that glorifies the Lord's name and shows that I receive and accept His love? For example, I am constantly working on my language during my speeches and seminars. When I get excited about something, my language can get colorful. Over the years I have gotten some negative feedback about it but had never really committed to improving this behavior until I suited up. It suddenly became apparent that my use of four-letter words didn't add a thing to my sessions, and it certainly didn't glorify the Lord's name. Besides, it set up an incongruity if I hoped to witness the power of the Lord in my life.

Once I committed to improving my language, do you think the change happened overnight? Absolutely not! Changing past behavior is not easy, because habit patterns encourage you to do certain things without even thinking. Keeping a journal has been helpful in tracking my progress. It helps me catch myself doing something right, allowing myself to pat myself on the back with a word of praise.

When you are learning to do something new—or in my case, unlearning a past behavior—you can't wait until you do it exactly right before you praise yourself. You have to praise progress because it is a moving target. Exactly right behavior is made up of a series of approximately right behaviors. So be kind to yourself. If you're not your own best friend, who will be?

What if I didn't make any progress? How would I record that in my journal? I would redirect myself. That means I would go back to goal setting and check my commitment. Self-praise should never prevent you from honestly evaluating your commitment to changing a negative behavior. Sometimes I even need to reprimand myself in my journal, but I do it and I don't dwell on it. That helps keep my mistakes in perspective: "I'm okay; it's just my behavior that's a problem sometimes." God didn't make junk. He just made real people who have behavior problems from time to time.

While keeping a journal is an excellent way to keep track of the things you do that are praiseworthy, there are other ways to praise yourself. Mostly it's a mindset—

thinking more about the good you do than the bad. It means recognizing that, for the most part, we really do try to spend more time lighting candles than cursing the darkness. It's just that it's so easy to get into the habit of focusing on your mistakes. The more you do that, the easier it is to stray off course and begin thinking you're all alone—that you need to do something great to earn your way into acceptance.

Remember, *you are already loved* but sometimes you need H.E.L.P. I have found that I stay on course much better when I am:

- Grounded in *H*umility
- Focused on my own sense of personal *E*xcellence—a balance between achieving and connecting
- Quiet and *L*istening to the voice that assures me, "You are the beloved."
- Accenting the positive and *P*raising God for my progress

While keeping *H*umility, *E*xcellence, *L*istening and *P*raising top of mind can be helpful, remember the ultimate help remains with Him. As Jesus promised at the end of Matthew:

> *And be sure of this: I am with you always,*
> *even to the end of the age.*
> Matthew 28:20

Jesus has not abdicated. He is there if we call and ready to help if we listen.

ONWARD AND UPWARD WITH ALL YOUR HEART

Trust in the Lord with all your heart
and lean not on your own understanding.
In all your ways acknowledge Him
and He shall direct your paths.

Proverbs 3:5-6

Easter now is my favorite holiday because it makes me realize how lucky I am to be a follower of Jesus. Why? Because my past is forgiven, my future is guaranteed and my present is secure in the unconditional love that God has given me through the grace of His Son.

While lowering my head and suiting up for the Lord by inviting God to enter my life took less than a minute, *that was only the beginning.* My focus moving forward is: How I can live my life each and every day as a true disciple of Jesus?

I have shared my vision for my life and my new emphasis on our Lead Like Jesus movement. The big question for me now is: How do I bring heaven down to earth and behave in such a way that God is happily able to say at the end of my earthly life, "Job well done, my good and faithful servant"?

A strategy that has helped me is to wake up and stay in the child-like mode, asking, "Daddy, where are we going today? What are we going to do?" Then I am open for the Lord to intervene at any time during the day if He has a better use of my time. I now am trying to live His purpose for my life, rather than my own.

That's all the advice I have to help you accept, receive and trust God's unconditional love. In fact, in many ways, this book is a meditation on God's unconditional love. I hope you have enjoyed it and found something of value in it. I have! Sometimes we teach what we most need to learn. I needed to write this book as much for me as for you. I needed this message and a reminder to rely on H.E.L.P. as much as anyone—particularly *help* from the Lord. While I have suited up and accepted God's grace, I still have to awaken constantly to His presence in my life so that I will trust increasingly in His unconditional love. I am certainly glad I am on His team.

In case you haven't suited up yet, I don't want to let you off the hook. Are you ready to receive God's unconditional love and accept His Son as your Savior? If you are, all you have to do is say and believe these words:

> "Lord, I come to You as a sinner—I fall
> short of 100. I realize I cannot reach 100 by
> myself. I need Your help. I accept Jesus into
> my life as my Savior, Lord, and Teacher. I
> humbly accept Your gift of grace and Your
> gift of salvation."

If you just suited up or were already on the team, great! If you didn't, you may be asking, "Is Jesus the only way to salvation and a better life on earth?"

I raised that very question one time with Norman Vincent Peale. I asked him, "Do you believe Jesus is the Truth and the Way?"

He said, "Absolutely!"

"But what about the millions of people who never heard about Jesus?" I wondered. "Or the millions of good people who heard about Him but decided not to follow Him?"

Norman smiled and said, "I believe in a loving God. I'll bet He handles that in a loving way. I'm in sales, not management."

While I like Norman's answer, I hope this question will never be a big issue for you, because you realize there is no better deal than suiting up for the Lord.

As you move from accepting to receiving to trusting, don't be too hard on yourself. It's not always easy to walk with Jesus. Every journey begins with a single step and moves along one step at a time. Those earthly voices you've listened to all your life can still get you off course. Keep seeking the H.E.L.P. you need—strive for *humility*, focus on your own *excellence*—not just achievement, keep *listening* to the voice that says, "You are the beloved," and *praise* your progress. And most important, remember: He who died for us is "with you always, to the very end of the age."

God loves you and so do I. Enjoy the trip!

ACKNOWLEDGMENTS

First, I am indebted to my soul mate, partner and teammate, Margie. I am so glad we both suited up and will be together forever. This in many ways is her story as much as mine. I also want to thank my son, Scott, and daughter, Debbie, for putting up with all my verbal and written spiritual ramblings for years. Their journey with the Lord is moving forward at different speeds but I am confident they know they are the beloved.

Since this is a new expanded version of my original *We Are the Beloved* published by Zondervan and then republished by The Blanchard Companies, I want to make sure I recognize people who contributed to both editions.

We Are the Beloved (1994)

I was fortunate to have many friends and colleagues who gave me feedback on the original version. In particular, I want to thank Jim Ballard and Sheldon Bowles for their very thoughtful and thorough feedback. It added a great deal to that edition.

A special thanks to my longtime secretary and friend, Eleanor Terndrup, and colleague, David Witt, for preparing and typing the various drafts of this manuscript with love, patience, and skill. Margret McBride, my literary agent and friend, was there once again to give me love, encouragement, and an all-win contract.

Lyn Cryderman, senior acquisitions editor at

Zondervan publishing house, was marvelous. He came to our cottage in upstate New York, plugged in his Macintosh, rolled up his sleeves, and spent two days with me finalizing the manuscript. I will forever be indebted to him.

It Takes Less Than One Minute to Suit Up for the Lord (2004)

I would have never committed to update my original book without the encouragement and support of my colleagues from the Center for *FaithWalk* Leadership and our Lead Like Jesus movement—Phyllis Hendry, Phil Hodges, Lee Ross and Vince Siciliano.

Nancy Jordan, part of my wonderful team at The Ken Blanchard Companies, shepherded every word in this manuscript with love, talent, dedication and an open and ever-ready-to-learn mind. This would have never happened without her help and prodding. Our colleague and writing partner, Martha Lawrence, gave us the benefit of her marvelous heart and skillful editorial talent.

Charlie "Tremendous" Jones insisted that I not only write a new updated and expanded edition of *We Are the Beloved* but that he and his wonderful folks at Executive Books would honcho its publication and distribution. Charlie is one of the greatest blessings in my life.

And finally, I want to acknowledge my three-member consulting team—The Father, the Son, and the Holy Spirit—for the energy and purpose They have given my life. I only hope I have represented You well in both editions.

BIBLIOGRAPHY

Blackaby, Henry. *Experiencing God Day by Day*. Nashville, TN: Broadman & Holman, 1998.

Blanchard, Kenneth and Norman Vincent Peale. *The Power of Ethical Management*. New York, NY: William Morrow, 1988.

_____, and Spencer Johnson. *The One-Minute Manager*. New York, NY: William Morrow, 1982.

_____, and Jesse Stoner. *Full Steam Ahead*. San Francisco, CA: Berrett-Koehler, 2003.

_____, and Sheldon Bowles, *Raving Fans*. New York, NY: William Morrow, 1993.

_____. and Sheldon Bowles *Gung Ho!* New York, NY: William Morrow, 1998.

Blanchard, Scott and Madeleine Homan. *Leverage Your Best, Ditch the Rest*. New York, NY: William Morrow, 2004.

Bolles, Richard N. *What Color Is Your Parachute?*. Berkeley, CA: Ten Speed Press, 1991.

_____, *How to Find Your Mission in Life*. Berkeley, CA: Ten Speed Press, 1991.

_____, *"Loving God and Loving Our Careers"* was an interview of Richard Bolles that appeared in "Crossings," a newsletter published by the Church of Divinity School of the Pacific, 1989.

Bright, Bill. *Four Spiritual Laws*. San Bernadino, CA: Campus Crusade for Christ International, 1965.

Buford, Bob. Co-author *Half Time*. Grand Rapids, MI: Zondervan, 1997.

Canfield, Jack and Hansen, Mark Victor. *Chicken Soup for the Soul*. Deerfield Beach, FL: Health Communications, Inc., 1993. I First read the "Sachi story" in this book. It originally came from page 48 of Dan Millman's book *Sacred Journey of the Peaceful Warrior*. Tiburon, CA: H.J. Kramer, Inc., 1983.

Collins, Jim. *Good to Great*. New York, NY: HarperCollins, 2001.

Crum, Thomas F. *The Magic of Conflict*. New York, NY: Simon & Schuster, 1988.

Hogan, Chuck. *Five Days to Golfing Excellence*. Sedona, AZ: T & C Publishing, 1986.

Howard, Vernon. *The Mystic Path of Cosmic Power*. Ojai, CA: New Life Foundation, 1988.

Hybels, Bill. *Honest to God?* Grand Rapids, MI: Zondervan, 1994.

_____, *Seven Wonders of the Spiritual World.* Irving, TX: Word, 1998.

Jones, Charlie "Tremendous", *Life Is Tremendous.* Wheaton, IL: Tyndale House, 1982.

Krushner, Harold S. *When Bad Things Happen to Good People.* Boston, MA: G.K. Hall, 1982.

_____, *When All You've Ever Wanted Isn't Enough.* Boston G.K.Hall, 1987.

Laidlow, Robert A. *The Reason Why.* Chattanooga, TN: Executive Books.

MacDonald, Gordon. *Ordering Your Private World.* Nashville, TN: Oliver-Nelson, 1985.

Nouwen, Henri J. M. and his thinking were introduced to me by Bob Buford. He sent me a tape of Nouwen's talk entitled "Solitude, Community, and Ministry" at the 1993 Foundation Conference for Christian Business Leaders in Toronto. After I finished the first draft of *We Are the Beloved*, a colleague found Nouwen's latest book, *Life of the Beloved* (New York, NY: Crossroad, 1992). Nouwen's work inspired the title for the first edition of this book.

Robbins, Anthony. *Unlimited Power*. New York, NY: Fawcett Books, 1987.

_____, *Awaken the Giant Within*. New York, NY: Summit, 1991.

Scherer, John with Larry Shook. *Work and the Human Spirit*. Spokane, WA: John Scherer & Associates, 1993.

Warren, Rick. Rick is the dynamic minister at Saddleback Valley Community Church in Southern California and author of *The Purpose Driven Life*. Bob Buford was the first to share with me Rick's approach to the spiritual journey of a Christian.

Ziglar, Zig. *See You at the Top*. Gretna, LA: Pelican Publishing Co., reprinted edition, 1982.

Zuck, Colleen (ed.). *The Daily Word*. Unity Village, MO: School of Christianity.

ABOUT THE AUTHOR

Ken Blanchard is the chief spiritual officer of The Ken Blanchard Companies, a worldwide human resource development company. He is also cofounder of the Center for *Faithwalk* Leadership, a nonprofit ministry dedicated to inspiring and educating people to Lead Like Jesus. Few people have made a more positive and lasting impact on the day-to-day management of people and companies as Ken Blanchard. He is the author of several bestselling books, including the blockbuster international bestseller *The One Minute* Manager and the giant business best-sellers *Raving Fans, Gung Ho!* and *Whale Done!*. His books have combined sales of more than fifteen million copies in more than twenty-five languages. He and his wife, Margie, live in San Diego and work with their son Scott, daughter Debbie, and Debbie's husband Humberto Medina.

SERVICES AVAILABLE

The Center for *FaithWalk* **Leadership** is a non-profit ministry dedicated to inspiring and equipping people to *Lead Like Jesus*. For more information on the Center for *FaithWalk* Leadership and its *Lead Like Jesus* simulcasts, seminars and resources, visit our website at www.leadlikeJesus.com.

The Center for *FaithWalk* Leadership
1229 Augusta West Parkway
Augusta, GA 30908
800-383-6890 or 706-863-8494
Fax 706-863-9372

The Ken Blanchard Companies is committed to helping people and organizations lead at a higher level. With a mission to *unleash the power and potential of people and organizations for the greater good*, the company is a global leader in workplace learning, productivity, and leadership effectiveness. To learn more, visit the Web site at www.kenblanchard.com or browse the eStore at www.kenblanchard.com/estore.

The Ken Blanchard Companies
125 State Place
Escondido, CA 92029
800 728-6000 or 760 489-5005
Fax: 760 489-8407